# Soapstone Car

# Beginners

*Step-By-Step Blueprint on How to Get Started in The World of Soapstone Carving For Complete Beginners (Including Beginner-Friendly Projects to Get You Started)*

# Introduction

Have you encountered carvings made of soapstone and loved how the art pieces looked, thus developing an interest in learning about soapstone carving?

Or,

Do you know a bit of carving, like wood or other carvings, but want to learn about soapstone carving to increase your skill set?

If you do, you came to the right place because this book has everything you need to know about soapstone carving.

Here is a brief history that will amuse you.

Soapstone, as so-called, has a soft nature. We can date soapstone carving as early as the Archaic archeological period between 8000BC to 1000BC. Communities have used soapstone from Africa to America, Asia to Australia to Europe in making historical statues, decorative items, and kitchen equipment.

For example, in Africa, the ancient Egyptians used soapstone to make scarab seals and amulets, while the Yoruba community of West Nigeria made soapstone statues of their heroes and heroines. The Native Americans also made kitchen equipment, cooking slabs, smoking pipes, and ornaments from soapstone.

The unique features of soapstone continue to make it the best choice for a wide variety of uses from then up to date. Today, the soapstone carvings market continues to grow as the number of people making these carvings has also grown to millions worldwide.

For so long, sculpture making has been seen as a highly complex thing for the talented, but the thing is that with the information in this book, you can make unique carvings.

In this book, you will learn:

- The various types of soapstone you can curve

- Which one to use in what kind of work

- The tools you will need

- The safety gear you must have

- How to make a few projects get you started

- And much more!

So, let's get started!

PS: I'd like your feedback. If you are happy with this book, please leave a review on Amazon.

Please leave a review for this book on Amazon by visiting the page below:

https://amzn.to/2VMR5qr

# Table of Contents

**Introduction** _____ **2**

**Chapter 1: What is Soapstone Carving** _____ **9**

Soapstone Carving _____ 11

The Principles of Carving _____ 13

**Chapter 2: Carving Tools** _____ **20**

1. Hand Tools _____ 20

2. Electronic Carving Tools _____ 30

How to Choose Tools for Your Project _____ 37

**Chapter 4: Safety Gear** _____ **39**

The Safety Wear _____ 39

The First Aid Kit _____ 41

Safety Precautions _____ 45

Carving Tools and Workspace Maintenance __ 48

**Chapter 5: The Carving Process** _____ **49**

1.  Select the Block of Soapstone _____ 49

2.  Prepare Your Workspace _____ 52

3.  Sketch the Pattern_____ 54

4.  Chipping Away the Outer layer _____ 55

5.  Carving with Files/Rasps _____ 56

6.  Round One sanding_____ 57

7.  Wet Sanding _____ 58

8.  Oil Polishing _____ 59

9.  Wax Polishing _____ 60

**Chapter 6: How to Carve a Soapstone Butterfly** _____**61**

Supplies:_____ 61

Instructions _____ 62

**Chapter 7: How to Carve African Traditional Stool** _____**71**

Requirements: _____ 71

Instructions _____72

## Chapter 8: How to Create a Hawk Carving Using Electronic Tools _____ 80

Supplies: _____ 80

Instructions: _____81

## Chapter 9: How to Carve a Soapstone Bear 89

Supplies: _____ 89

Instructions: _____ 90

## Chapter 10: How to Make a Soapstone Cooking Pot _____ 94

Supplies: _____ 94

Instructions: _____ 95

## Chapter 11: Carving a Soapstone Tortoise 98

Supplies: _____ 98

Instructions: _____ 99

## Chapter 12: Carving a Soapstone Rabbit 102

Supplies:_____ 102

Instructions: _____ 103

## Chapter 13: Carving Soapstone Coasters _106

Supplies:_____ 106

Instructions: _____ 106

## Chapter 14: Carving a Soapstone Egg ____109

Supplies:_____ 109

Instructions: _____110

## Chapter 15: Carving a Soapstone Candle Holder_____ 113

Supplies:_____113

Instructions: _____114

## Conclusion_____ 116

# Chapter 1: What is Soapstone Carving

In this chapter, you will learn what soap carving is, but first, let us start by understanding what carving entails.

***Carving*** is a subtractive sculpting technique that involves chipping away at a block of material until you get your desired shape. It is a three-dimensional artwork categorized under subtractive sculpturing since you will start with a block of material and use your tools to trim it to your desired shape or object.

In simple terms, carving refers to shaping a material block into an object. The different materials you can carve are endless, but some of them include wood, stones, soap, soapstone, and marble.

Below are examples of carvings:

*Image 1.1: Lion carving*

*Image 1.2: A fishing bear carving*

**Note**: In this book, we will focus on carving soapstone, but with this skill, you can also carve wood, soap, or stone.

# Soapstone Carving

**Soapstone** is a *malleable metamorphic rock rich in minerals, especially magnesium, and talc.* Its malleability results from the high talc content, enabling it to be used in carving for a long time.

Since the talc content in soapstone varies widely, the softness of soapstone is not uniform but varies. Soapstone also comes in different colors, ranging from cream white, light pink, and grey hue to even black colors.

Besides carving, soapstone is also used as an insulator in electrical components and housing.

## Types of Soapstone

There are various types of soapstones with distinct features varying from hardness to their color. Knowing these multiple types with their components is essential to use them appropriately.

Below are types of soapstone according to their hardness:

- **Talc Soapstone**

Talc soapstone is the **softest type of all**. It is soft such that you can scratch it with your fingernails. The softness makes it the least durable soapstone. Therefore, it is ideal for creating indoor decorative carvings that are small in size and kids' toys.

Since it is not as durable, we can use it for short-term carvings, such as event decoration items.

- **Steatite Soapstone**

Steatite is **more rigid than talc but not so hard**. It lasts relatively longer. This stone is, therefore, ideal for indoor decorative items. Steatite soapstone can last longer if used to make immovable massive indoor carvings.

- **Chlorite Soapstone**

This rock is the **most rigid version of soapstone** and the most durable one. Therefore, it is the most appropriate choice for carving enormous outdoor carvings, as they can withstand extreme weather changes. Being the hardest, it is also ideal for making carvings meant to move from place to place.

# The Principles of Carving

Knowing how to carve will allow you to create gorgeous pieces of work that you can use to decorate different spaces. However, to learn how to make beautiful objects effectively, you will require a creative mind and skill of the hand, and some artistic knowledge/principles to guide you.

So,

It is crucial to understand these principles before we pick our tools and trim our material block.

Below are some basic principles you must understand as a beginner to learn to carve successfully:

## 1. Ratio

*Ratio*, which we also refer to as **proportion**, *dictates that the elements of your work must be comparable in quantity, size, and degree of emphasis.* This principle will help you show the relationship between the different parts of your product. To create a carving, you must first have a clear view of the most common proportions of the features of the original object you want to carve.

For instance, if you were carving your soapstone into the shape of a dog, you must ensure that the parts of your product are proportional.

However, this can change depending on the message you intend to communicate with your artwork, which may give some variations in emphasis. But under normal circumstances, your dog's legs should not appear longer than the neck, or you have a more oversized neck with a smaller head.

So, in other words, your product is supposed to be proportional.

And,

As you start carving, you must focus on the most common items to help you get the inner details right. The standard proportions will draw attention to the finer individual features.

## 2. Articulation

*Articulation* is *expressing your idea in a form that others can understand*. This means that your carving **should be understandable**. If your work is an inspiration and you want to communicate the message, your carving should clearly articulate your message correctly and effectively.

In other words, your work should communicate your message to others. Even if it is not an inspired work, your product is supposed to be easily identifiable. For example, when carving a dog, make it easy to know that it is a dog, not a bear.

## 3. Scale

The principle of scale states that *your carving should align with the scale of its environment.* So, knowing where you will use or put this carving is imperative before you make an object. This means that you will have to consider if your carving is best placed outdoors or indoors or if it will be just a single element in a large complex like a building, in which case the size of your carving should be in scale with the rest of the objects.

For example, an outdoor carving will look more extensive than the one you would want on your TV stand. Also, the carving at a shopping mall's entrance must be larger than the one you use in your house.

Therefore, ensure to make your carving into the correct scale so that we can notice it for it to be effective.

## 4. Balance

The principle of balance is *about your carving's stability or freestanding and equilibrium.* In carving and sculpturing, we will look at the balance principle in three aspects:

✓ *The physical stability*

Physical stability is *the ability of the carving to stand on its own* without support, resulting from natural balance. Unlike tall and straight carvings, this balance is easy to achieve with four-legged animals and objects with wider bases.

Therefore, ensure that your carving achieves actual physical stability.

✓ *Compositional balance*

Compositional balance or equilibrium is *about weight distribution and forces' interaction within your carving.*

All natural objects we tend to carve always have an even distribution of weight within themselves, which is why they have stability.

So, as you will be making forms of these natural beings in carving, you must ensure that your final product has an even distribution of weight that will give it balance.

#### ✓ *Subtle placement*

When carving objects that may be challenging to balance on their own, you can *achieve balance by modifying them* to make them balance.

For example, when making a human carving that cannot balance on its own, you can change it so that it will stand. In such a case, you can include the ground on which it stands to increase the base, make a walking stick to support stability, or create the carving while leaning on a tree to achieve stability. These ways will help you achieve balance while making the carving beautiful. So as you make human carvings, it is advisable to apply subtle placement and other options of relaxation and tension application to achieve balance since your carving will not be moving, nor will it adjust any muscles.

## 5. Orientation

The orientation principle will *help you understand and describe the positioning of parts of your carving with each other or the poses you will employ in your carving.* It requires some spatial scheme to guide the positioning of parts of the carving regarding the **Axis** and **Plane** systems of your carving.

For example, the orientation principle will help you decide on the right pose for living beings' carvings and how to position components on the other objects you want to carve.

But what do the Axis and Plane mean?

## Planes

In carving and entire sculpturing, these are imaginary planes to which the surfaces, axes, direction of volumes, and positions are referred. There are four planes for three dimension artwork such as carving.

They include:

✓ Horizontal planes

✓ Frontal planes

✓ Two profile planes

These *planes give the guidelines to help you place the various parts of your carving in the proper position and help you create pauses that achieve balance.*

## Axis

Axis is *an imaginary line at an object's center that suggests its mass's gravitational pivot.* This imaginary line runs through or near a proportional arrangement volume or group of volumes. Bodies with various parts have several axes in their entire body, while the straight, upright body has a single axis running from top to bottom.

With the positioning of parts, the poses of your carving, and spatial compositions in carving, you will have to formulate them regarding the four planes and the axes.

Carving without the idea of the planes and axes of the object you want to make will result in the unreasonable positioning of parts of the carving. For example, if you are making a human carving, the planes, and the axes will help you place the hands appropriately, without which the hand might end up being lower than the shoulder or have an imbalanced carving.

The principle of orientation will also help you achieve balance in your carving.

These principles and many others, such as contrast, color, harmony, and continuity, are compositional tools that will help you make carvings that are very attractive and harmonious to their environment.

Let us now look at the tools you will need to carve.

# Chapter 2: Carving Tools

Soapstone carving, as we learned earlier, is a subtractive sculpturing method. Subtractive in the sense that it involves chipping off the block of the soapstone until you get your desired product. This means that you will need special tools to achieve this.

Below are some of the primary and easily accessible tools you need to carve:

## 1. Hand Tools

- ## Chisel

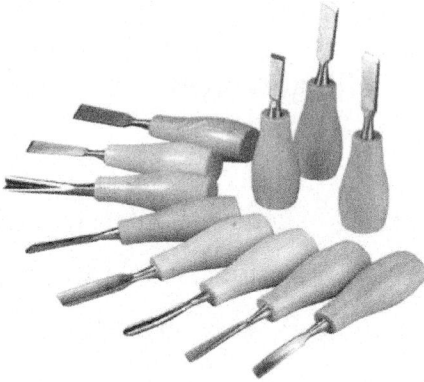

*Image 2.1: chisels*

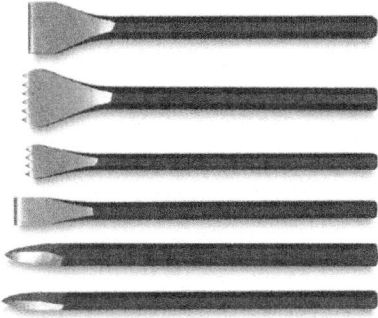

*Image 2.2: Chisels*

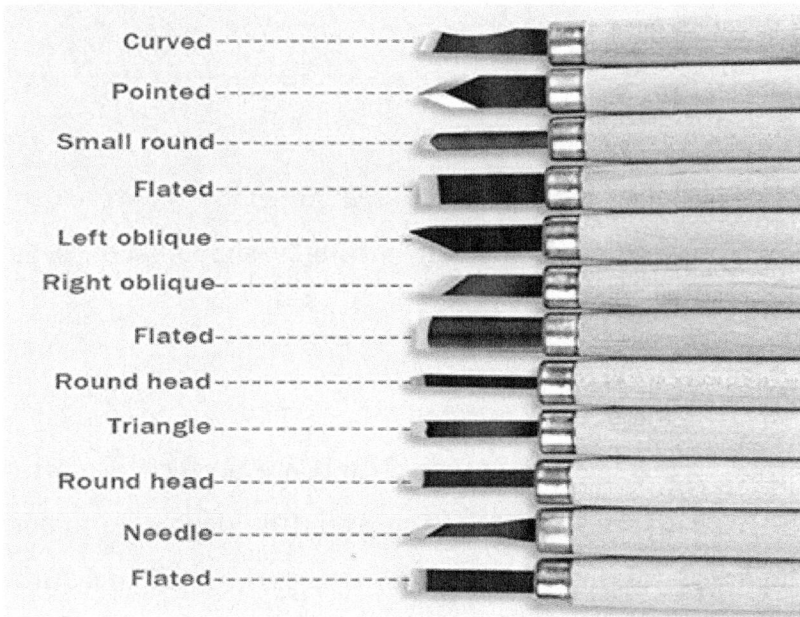

## Image2.3: types of chisels

A chisel is used to *chop out the parts of the soapstone* block as you reduce it into your desired shape.

There are various types of chisels with specific functions in the carving process. As you can see in the images above, these chisels have different shapes and patterns at their cutting edge.

**The flat chisel** is the most common in most workshops, used to chip away the unwanted parts of the material. In image 2.2 above, a flat chisel is the first one from the top.

Other types of chisel include:

### Diamond chisel

This chisel has a diamond/triangular shape on its cutting edge. You will need it when cutting V-shape grooves and when cleaning corners.

### Corner chisel

As the name suggests, corner chisels are perfect for cutting corners. Their edge is right-angled (90 degrees), making them ideal for making perfect corners without measuring tools.

### Lathe chisel

Lathe chisels are used to shape products and are common in wood carving.

## *Power chisel*

Power chisels are the modern types that use a motor to power, meaning you will not use a hammer to hit on it. This chisel is more efficient and accurate compared to the manual one. Also, where you need to apply more energy while chipping, the power chisel will significantly help.

There are over 20 types of chisels to explore depending on the shape of their cutting edge. The above discussed are just a few to help you understand that specific chisels exist for particular functions.

## Tips on How to Use a Chisel

✓ Ensure that you properly mark the soapstone you want to carve.

✓ Always use your left hand to hold the chisel while the right hand has the hammer

✓ Place the chisel's cutting edge on the marked line properly, and strike the harmer on the head of the chisel. Before hitting the second blow, reset your chisel.

✓ As you use the chisel, focus on the cutting edge.

✓ It would be best to have the hammer hit the center of the chisel's head.

- **Hammer**

*Image 2.4: Hammer*

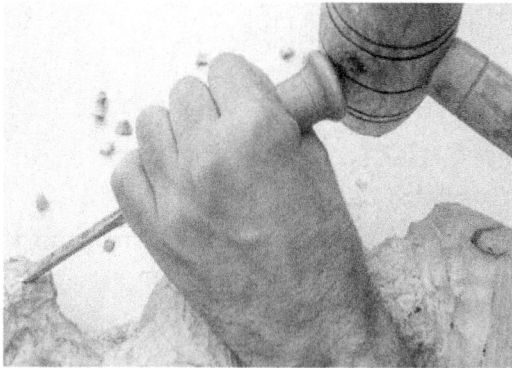

*Image 2.5: Wooden hammer*

You will need a hammer to use with the chisel.

How?

When chipping away the soapstone to the shape of your desired carving, you will use the hammer to hit on the chisel.

Hammers are in different sizes to provide the weights needed for their specific use. Most common hammers have metallic heads, but there are still hammers with wooden ones.

## • **Pencil**

A pencil is for marking the soapstone before you start to chip away.

Before you start carving, you must draw the shape of your desired object. The markings act as the guidance or the plan for achieving your desired carving.

## • **Sculpting Knife**

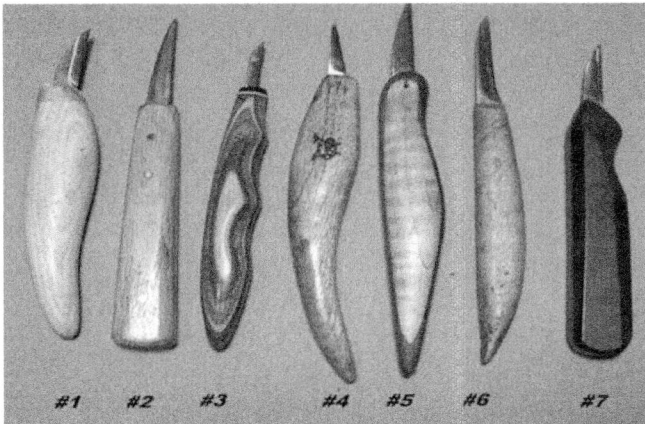

*Image 2.6: Soapstone carving knives*

It is essential to have a sculpting knife always in your tool kit. This knife is beneficial as you will need it to make a cut, chip away thin slices of your material as your carving takes shape or mark lines on your block.

These knives are always very sharp since you must apply a lot of pressure or force to carve soapstone. Therefore, reminding you to be very careful lest you cut yourself is crucial.

- **Rasp**

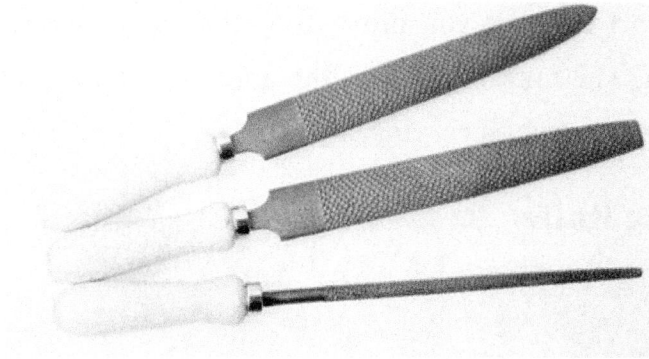

*Image 2.7: Rasps*

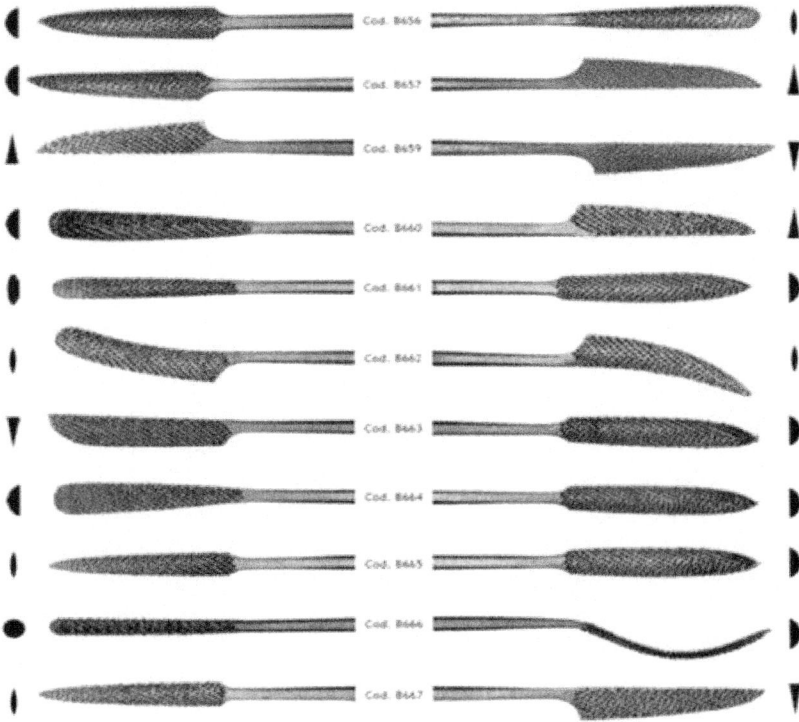

*Image 2.8: Double-sided rasps*

Rasps are tools that help reduce and shape to leave a smooth surface ready for finishing or further carving. There are a variety of rasps;- some rough and some finer than others. This means that the level or stage your work is in will determine the rasp you will use.

The double-sided rasps are designed to fasten and make the work more accessible for the artists in carving since it is much easier and faster to flip the tool on the hand than drop one rasp to select another.

- **Calipers**

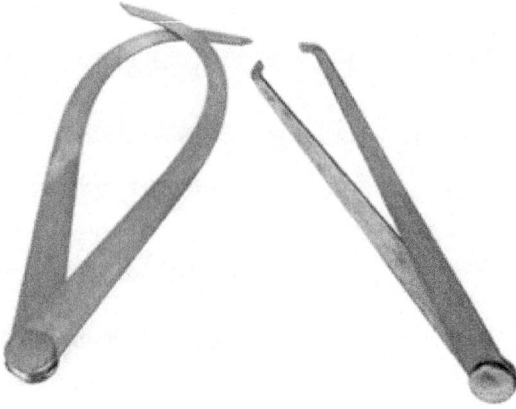

*Image 2.9: Calipers*

Calipers are measuring tools in carving. When carving a live object, calipers will help you have the exact measurements of your work, allowing you to enlarge it or reduce it to scale on your carving.

- **Sandpaper**

*Image 2.10: Sandpaper*

Sandpaper is a refining tool. After the finest rasp, you will then use the sandpaper to scrub on your object to get a smoother surface.

Sandpaper is also made in various roughness for different finishing levels, and as you begin the refining, you will start with the roughest as you change until you finally get to the finest. This tool eliminates the scratches left behind by the files or the rasps.

- **Sharpening Tools**

These include sharpening stones and files. These tools will help you hone the sculpting knives and the chisel.

- **Wax/Oil**

Oil or wax is used in the final stage of the carving. After refining, you apply wax or oil to make your carving sparkle. Also, waxing and oiling help in giving your carving color.

## 2. Electronic Carving Tools

Besides hand tools, you can also use electronic instruments to do the work more efficiently and faster.

Let's learn about some electronic tools:

- **Grinders**

Grinders are used for cutting, shaping, and refining, making carving much faster and easier.

Below are examples of grinders:

# 1) *Variable Speed Angle Grinder*

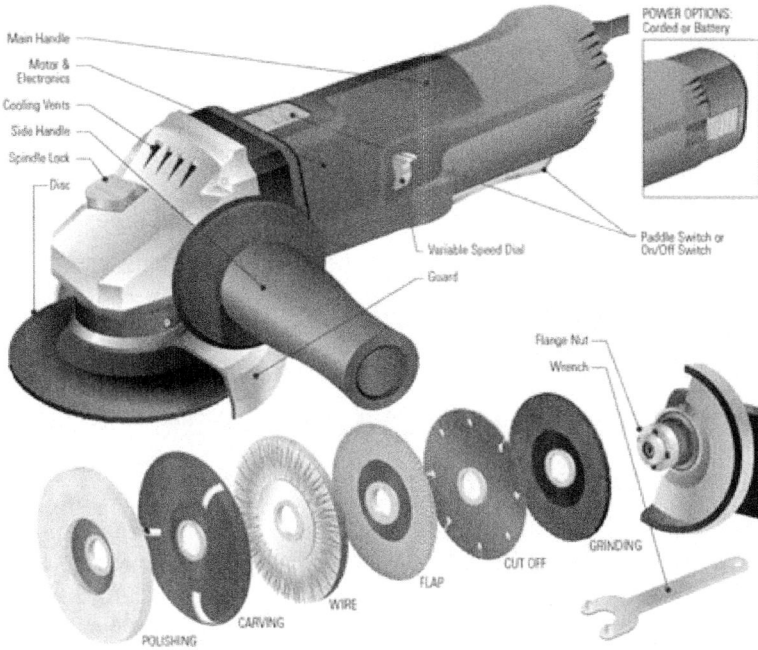

Main Handle

Motor &
Electronics

Cooling Vents

Side Handle

Spindle Lock

Disc

POWER OPTIONS:
Corded or Battery

Paddle Switch or
On/Off Switch

Variable Speed Dial

Guard

Flange Nut

Wrench

GRINDING

CUT OFF

FLAP

WIRE

CARVING

POLISHING

*Image 3.1:Mikita angle grinder*

An angle grinder is one of the essential electronic tools for carving. It is used to do most basic carving activities, like cutting, chipping away, shaping, sanding, and even waxing. There are full-speed angle grinders, but using a variable-speed grinder is advisable to ease your work and help you reduce the speed in situations requiring minimal vibration.

The function of this angle grinder depends on the head attached to it. The following are some of the components you will need to connect to the angle grinder for the various functions:

✓ ***Braised diamond blade***

A braised diamond blade is ideal for cutting away vast chunks of material and making initial cuts. Also, this blade has the slightest vibration, making it suitable for making cuts in the most sensitive parts of the carving without breaking them, like a thin tail of an animal carving.

This blade comes in different sizes, so what you will need to use will depend on the amount of material you want to chip away or the depth of the cut you want to make. Larger blades help chip out a large amount of soapstone faster and are excellent for making deep cuts.

✓ ***Sintered cutter blade***

Sintered cutter blades have rough surfaces, giving them higher vibration than braised diamond blades. This blade is used for cutting a massive amount of material, and the rough texture makes it ideal for grinding and shaping.

## *How to Use a Variable Speed Grinder*

First, this being an electronic tool, you must have a suitable power source. You can use batteries or connect the grinder directly to an electric power supply socket.

To start using this grinder:

✓ Fix the blade in the head. To do this, select the knife you want to use. Using a wrench, loosen the range nut to remove it, then fit the blade in and fasten it using the range nut back. **Note**: Disconnect the grinder from the power source as you fix or change the edge.

✓ After fitting the blade, connect the grinder to the power source and switch it on. Before switching it on, set the variable speed dial to the slowest speed end (point zero). The switch buttons have a lock position primarily so that you don't have to hold on to the controller as you use the grinder to keep it on.

✓ Once your grinder is on, please set it to your desired speed, depending on what you want to do. It is always advisable not to use full speed. Hold the grinder firmly with one hand and use your free hand to hold it on the side handle. Let it reach the full speed you set before landing it on the soapstone.

✓ Hold the grinder at an angle and let it land on the soapstone gently to avoid injuries. Do not press the grinder so hard on the surface of the soapstone to prevent over-cutting and injuries. **Note**: You must wear all the protective outfits while carving with a grinder since it involves dust and chipped-away stones falling so fast. It would help to keep your other tools together in a raised place lest you lose them in the dust.

### 2) Variable Die Grinder

Image 3.2: Variable die grinder

The variable die grinder is another primary carving tool that does much work in the carving process. After cutting using the angle grinder, the die grinder takes up the role of shaping the material into a carving. This grinder is ideal for shaping since it can get into hard-to-reach parts of the carving.

The die grinder uses burrs to chip away the soapstone. The burrs come in various shapes to get into those hard-to-reach places and form and shape specific carving parts.

Besides shaping, you can also fix a buffing wheel on the die grinder to apply wax in the finishing process.

### 3) *Variable Speed Dremel*

*Image 3.3:Hilda variable speed Dremel*

Dremel is a refining tool. After the carving has taken its basic shape, you get a Dremel to bring out the finer details of your carving. This tool uses burrs that are much smaller compared to the ones for the die grinder.

### How to Use Dremel in Carving

Just as in the case of the grinder, the Dremel uses electric power to function.

So,

✓ The first step is to ensure that you have an excellent electric power source. And before connecting it to the power source, select the burr to use and fit it on the chuck of the machine.

✓ Connect the Dremel to the power source and switch it on. Set the speed to use using the speed control button and let it reach the whole set speed before landing it on the soapstone to start carving with it. Once it is set and ready, hold it with one hand on the body and the other hand closer to the burr and let it have a light touch on the carving.

This machine also uses small cutting discs to make the small finishing cuttings on the carving, like making patterns and shaping the small parts.

These electronic tools can cause serious injuries when poorly handled. You must therefore be very careful while using them.

## How to Choose Tools for Your Project

As we have learned, there are several tools you can choose for your carving set. Some, like the rasps and sandpaper, will likely be used in any project. However, there are some that you will use under certain factors.

Here are some of the factors you need to consider when deciding on the carving tool to use in your project:

- **Size of the Carving**

The desired carving size you want is an essential factor when selecting the tools. Electronic tools are ideal for large projects, while hand tools are most appropriate for small projects. Also, if making minimal carvings like a toy-size butterfly, you will not need a chisel and a hammer, as the sculpting knife will be enough.

- **Type of the Soapstone**

The type and size of the soapstone you are working on also matter. The grinders are the most appropriate when working on a vast chlorite soapstone. On the other hand, a chisel with a hammer or a sculpting knife will be okay for talc soapstone.

Other factors include the availability of the power source and the available tools to choose from, among many other factors.

# Chapter 4: Safety Gear

## The Safety Wear

Soapstone carving involves a lot of dust emission, with large and small particles of the stone falling or flying around. Therefore, as an artist, you must protect yourself from injuries, which means you must dress appropriately for the job.

The following are some of the safety items you will need to have:

- **Cap/helmet**

*Image 2.11: Caps and helmet*

You will need either a mavin cap or a helmet to prevent specks of dust and stone particles from reaching your hair.

- **Safety Glasses**

Safety glasses are for protecting your eyes from dust and possible injuries.

- **Dust Masks**

*Image 2.12: Dust masks*

Dust masks are for covering your nose and mouth to protect you from inhaling clouds of dust, which may cause respiratory complications.

If you are using the grinders, you will also need ear masks to protect your ears from the noise that can affect your hearing.

- **Apron**

An apron will protect you from dust. Also, some aprons are made with pockets that you can use to select and put the light tools you will need in the process for easier access.

- **Hand Gloves**

Hand gloves will protect your hand from severe injuries.

- **Safety Boots**

If you're using a raised stand, you will need safety boots to protect your feet from falling parts of the soapstone during cutting and chipping away.

## The First Aid Kit

As you carve, you are susceptible to injuries such as cuts, breakage, dust particles getting into your eyes, electrocution, etc. Therefore, having a well-equipped first aid kit in your workspace/workshop is necessary.

A well-established workshop should have more than one first aid kit well distributed in the room for easy access.

And,

As a beginner, always ensure that your kit has the following essential components well-arranged in the box:

- **Sterile Eye Wash**

Sterile eyewash is for washing your eyes when dust or small particles enter your eyes during carving.

- **Sterile Cleansing Wipes**

These wipes are for cleaning wounds if/when you get cut. Ensure that you do not clean your wound with any material that is not sterile.

- **Sterile Dressings**

Sterile dressings are for dressing wounds. They come in various sizes to cater to injuries of different sizes.

- **Plasters/Sterile Plasters**

These plasters help close the wound.

- **Antiseptic Cream**

This cream is helpful in cleansing and protecting minor wounds from infections. It also treats skin reactions.

- **Clotting Sponge**

The clotting sponge is another primary component. This sponge will help you stop bleeding. Ensure that you have several of these sponges.

- **Bandages**

After cleaning and treating your wound, you must dress it to prevent further infections. Besides the sterile dressings, bandages are instrumental in dressing wounds, especially significant ones.

- **Non-adherent Dressing Pads**

These pads are put on the wound before bandaging to help prevent the bandage from sticking to the injury.

- **Micropore Surgical Tape**

Micropore surgical tape helps close wounds and stick the bandage.

- **DIY Tourniquets**

These are for tying the arms or the legs to stop blood flow.

You can buy tourniquets, but a homemade one is advisable for quality. Also, please note that tourniquets are only for arms and legs; do not use them on body parts like the neck.

- **Safety Pins**

Safety pins are for sticking the bandage after dressing the wound.

- **A Pair of Scissors**

Scissors are for cutting bandages and opening the packaging of these components.

- **Emergency Medical Pamphlet**

This component is rarely used but is an important one. It is a reference book that helps you conduct first aid correctly.

The above-listed items are just a few of the endless list of components a first aid kit should have.

**Note:**

✓ Your workstation should have at least two first aid kits. Keep one on the ground level for easy access even when you fall on the ground and cannot get up.

✓ Please do not keep the first aid kit components in their packages. Remove them from the boxes in which they come. Only use the container that keeps them sterile.

✓ Always keep your phone on and close to you. Ensure that you keep the emergency contacts easily accessible.

✓ Ensure you undertake first aid training courses. Also, if you are working with a team, they must be trained too.

✓ To quickly get any components from the first aid box, empty the whole content on a surface and spread them to get what you are looking for much faster.

## Safety Precautions

Just like in every workshop, there are dangers and injuries that you will be prone to as you carve. Therefore, there are safety measures that you must take into account to complete your work safely.

Let us have a look at some of the basic safety precautions:

- **Ensure Your Workshop has Enough Space for The Job and is As Free From Hazards As Possible**

If you use an enclosed room, ensure it has a sound ventilation system, free from flooding. Since soapstone carving involves a lot of dust, an open-air workspace is much better.

- **Keep Your Tools, All Your Guards, and Shields In Place**

The guards, shields, and tools should be kept strategically for easy access. This will help increase efficiency and keep you from harm and injuries.

- **Put on The Personal Protective Gear Listed Above Always**

Never, ever start working without putting on your protective gear. Your safety should be the priority always.

- **Ensure You Have Adequate Lighting**

The lighting system should enable you to see well to avoid injuries.

- **Ensure Your Tools are in Good Condition**

For example, a hammer that has a cracked handle can injure you easily.

- **Protect Yourself from Electrocution or Electric Shock**

Fit safety switches on your power tools and avoid contact or using naked wires.

- **Have Your First Aid Kits**

Ensure your first aid kits are well equipped and strategically placed in the workspace.

- **As you carve:**

✓ Maintain secure footing and balance

✓ Use each tool for its appropriate function

✓ Ensure that you keep your tools in safe places during carving

✓ Use each tool at its speed, do not force any tool

✓ Give your full attention to the process

✓ Whenever your power chisel or any power tool jams, immediately turn off the power switch

✓ Handle the sharp tools with ultimate care to avoid cuts

✓ Do not use tools without handles or those with cracked handles

✓ Switch off the electronic equipment that is not in use

✓ Disconnect the electronic equipment from the power source completely when changing the burrs or the blades

# Carving Tools and Workspace Maintenance

To maintain your tools and workspace:

✓ Please clean up your tools after use before you store them.

✓ Ensure to sharpen the cutting tools before storage.

✓ Keep all your power tools safe and secure to avoid damage and unauthorized use.

✓ Repair any slight damage to your equipment and replace damaged or used-up parts.

✓ Keep your workstation clean after closing the day's job.

# Chapter 5: The Carving Process

Now that you know the tools you will need to carve and the safety measures to implement, let us get to the process before we get to the start-up projects.

Below is the carving process flow:

## 1. Select the Block of Soapstone

The first step of carving soapstone is to select the block of the soapstone you will use as your material. As we learned earlier, soapstone is not a uniform material, and depending on the carving you want to make, it is essential to consider the following as you make your selection:

- **Size**

The size of the soapstone block will depend on the carving size you want to make. Sometimes the live object you wish to make its carving also determines the block size you need.

For example, if you want to make a giant lion carving that is to be placed at the entrance of a shopping mall, then you will need to select a big soapstone block. The carving must be big enough to be noticeable. At this point, we consider the principle of scale.

On the other hand, having a small soapstone is suitable if you want to make small carvings.

Considering the size will help you save time and minimize material waste. Soapstone is not a cheap material, so reducing waste is economically essential.

- **Color**

Soapstone comes in various colors. It is crucial to consider the color, depending on what you want to carve.

For example, black will look perfect on a penguin carving than yellow, while grey will look better on a bear or dog carving than a human carving.

Also, the places where the carving will be placed also determine the color selection. A black block of soapstone will not fit a carving of an angel to be placed at the sanctuary's entrance.

- **The Softness of the Soapstone**

Depending on your desired size and shape of the carving, it is necessary to consider the softness of the soapstone to use.

As we learned in our first chapter, soapstones vary in softness; some are harder than others.

So, how do you choose a soapstone regarding softness?

It is advisable to use the harder soapstone to make enormous carvings, while for small sizes like a toy butterfly, softer soapstone will be okay.

- **The Place to Use the Carving**

When picking the soapstone, you must also consider the space your carving will decorate. A vast carving for displaying in an open-air area will require chlorite soapstone, whereas a small carving for your living room decoration will not necessarily need this hardest soapstone.

- **Cost**

As you decide on the soapstone, it is vital to consider the amount of money you will spend in acquiring the stone against the gain.

The client will also determine the soapstone when you become a professional and make your carving commercial. Prestigious clients go for ostentation goods and will prefer the most expensive soapstone carving.

## 2. Prepare Your Workspace

After choosing the soapstone block through considering the factors, the second thing to do is to put your workspace in order. During this step, you will select where you will work from, provide all the supplies, and arrange them in order.

You need to do the following as part of preparing your workspace:

- **Select the Space**

Choose where you will be carving; in a room or an open-air space. However, ensure the fixtures and fittings are in place. For example, if you use a raised stand, workbench, and such, ensure they are already set for use.

If your workspace is in a room, ensure good ventilation since soapstone carving involves a lot of dust.

- **Arrange the Supplies and Tools**

To do this:

✓ Arrange your supplies, starting with the block of soapstone you will work on, the tools you need, and even the risk management tools.

✓ Ensure that your tools are not scattered on the floor to prevent injuries and their loss in the dust. Keep the tools in a position, preferably in a raised place, where you can access them easily when carving.

✓ Fix the power supply with the safety switch to prevent you from electrification.

✓ Position the first aid kit(s).

- **Check on the Lighting**

If you are carving in a room, ensure that it has sufficient light that will help you see clearly. Working in an open-air space during the day will require no particular lighting system.

As you prepare the workspace, wear protective clothing, and prepare yourself for the work.

Also, ensure that you have enough water in place.

## 3. Sketch the Pattern

In a well-arranged workplace with the soapstone block in position, the next thing is to sketch the pattern of your desired carving on the block.

Here is how to do this:

✓ Draw the object you want to curve on the soapstone using the pencil. These marks will guide you as you start carving, as it is on that mark that you will put your chisel. It is challenging to begin cutting from nowhere without the guiding lines on the block. Earlier on, we learned that you could also use the sculpting knife to do the marking. However, using a pencil to sketch is advisable since you can make changes by erasing and drawing again when you don't get it right.

✓ After you confirm the sketch pattern, you can use the knife to make the marks more visible and permanent. Pencil marks may get erased in the process due to the touching and dusting, while the knife marks will remain traceable.

And,

As you make the sketch, consider the shape of the carving you want to make and that of the soapstone.

Also, be keen on the illustration on all the sides of the soapstone block. In most cases, if not all, each side of the soapstone will always have a different sketch. For example, suppose you want to carve a cup out of a cuboid block of soapstone. In that case, the upper surface will have a circular sketch, and the bottom surface opposite the upper surface should have another circular graphic but a smaller circle than the one on the upper surface. Also, the side hosting the handle will have a different sketch from the other three.

## 4. Chipping Away the Outer layer

After the sketching, you can start carving by chipping away the unwanted outer layer as you follow the sketch. Depending on the size of your block of soapstone, you can use a chisel and a hammer or the sculpting knife to chip away the soapstone around the sketch outline.

The tool you will use at this stage will also depend on the type of soapstone you are carving.

For example, starting to carve a large block of chlorite soapstone will require a chisel and a hammer, while making a butterfly carving from a small talc soapstone will not need a chisel; a sculpting knife will be applicable.

As you chip away the outer layer:

✓ Ensure you carve following the guidelines sketched on all the sides of the soapstone.

✓ Ensure that you chip all the sides simultaneously without ignoring any of the sides.

✓ Stop after every three to four cuts to check if you are still within the guidelines until your carving takes the basic shape.

## 5. Carving with Files/Rasps

The basic shape from chipping will come with rough surfaces and edges. At this point, you will use the rasps to do away with the roughness.

At this stage:

✓ First, use the sculpting knife to cut thin slices off until it looks finer, and then use the rasps, starting with the roughest one.

✓ Use the rasp to scratch the surface of the carving. Besides doing away with the roughness, the course rasp will also help you get to the shape of your carving.

✓ When you finish scratching with the roughest rasp, you will get a fair shape, but the carving will still have rough scratches. Pick the next rasp, which is finer than the one you used, and scratch the carving, then move to the next one until you use the finest one. After this, you should have a definite shape of the carving ready for finishing.

# 6. Round One sanding

Sanding will help remove the scratches left behind by the rasps.

To do this:

✓ Pick your roughest sandpaper of all and scrub the whole carving. As you do the sanding, you are supposed to tell that the surface is getting smoother.

✓ Once you have sanded the whole carving, pick finer sandpaper and do the same for filing round two. Move to the next one until you get to the finest sandpaper. You will tell that the carving is smooth once the scratches from the previous step are gone. You will also feel it with your hand.

## 7. Wet Sanding

At this stage, you can use either two grit sandpapers or even one could be enough.

For this step:

✓ Fill your basin with water; wet your carving and the sandpaper(s) and start sanding.

As you do this, you will notice that the sanding gunk will build up while your carving becomes marble-like and smooth. Continue until you are satisfied with the smoothness of the surfaces.

Be careful to sand the whole carving evenly lest you change the form or shape of your carving.

When you get to this stage, you can remove some of your protective gear, like the helmet, the safety glasses, and the dust masks.

# 8. Oil Polishing

Once you are satisfied with the outcome of the wet sanding, dry up the carving before applying oil to it.

Danish oil, Tung oil, boiled linseed oil, and double-boiled linseed oil, among many others, are the most common to polish a soapstone carving.

And to oil polish your work:

✓ Wipe a thin coat of the oil on the carving using your hand or a soft cloth. However, avoid applying excess oil, as it will make the carving gummy and too hard to polish.

Soapstone has the capability of absorbing oil. Rub the oil on the carving; the heat from the friction between your hand and the carving will facilitate the oil absorption.

Also, since soapstone tends to change color when it absorbs the oil, it will be effortless to know where you might have missed while applying the oil. Rub the carving while adding oil until you are happy with the look.

Applying oil or wax is meant to make the carving sparkle to look more beautiful.

From this point, your carving will be ready, but still, you can decorate by painting if you wish.

# 9. Wax Polishing

Soapstone carving can also be polished using beeswax, besides oil.

To polish using beeswax:

✓ Put your carving into an oven and heat it to between 120°C to 150°C. As much as soapstone can sustain up to above 900°C without any adverse effect, do not exceed 150°C for waxing. That is because heating above these temperatures will cause the beeswax to evaporate instead of polishing the carving.

✓ Remove the carving from the oven and hold the beeswax against the hot soapstone to melt. Spread the wax on the carving until every part is waxed, then let it cool.

✓ The wax will also cool and solidify as the carving cools, dulling the shiny carving. Therefore, use a cloth to wipe down the excess polish on the carving to bring out the shiny surface, then let the carving fully cool.

Now, let us look at some practical exercises to start your carving journey with.

# Chapter 6: How to Carve a Soapstone Butterfly

Having learned the tools, the safety gears, and the carving process, let's start making a butterfly carving as our first practical exercise.

## Supplies:

✓ Small talc soapstone (6cm by 5cm by 1cm)

✓ Pencil

✓ A sculpting knife

✓ Rasps

✓ Sandpapers

✓ Thin wire

✓ Glue

✓ Basin

✓ Water

## Instructions

Since we are making a small butterfly carving, we will not need stands, workbenches, or a big workshop. However, you will still need to put your tools together and in a place where you can reach them easily.

Also, protective gear like dust masks and glasses may not be essential since this carving will not emit much dust compared to a power chisel. But you can just put them on, just in case.

One essential thing you **must wear is hand gloves** since your hand will be the workbench. You will be holding the block in one hand as you chip away using your other hand with a sculpting knife. Therefore, wear gloves to avoid cutting your hand as you carve.

## Steps to Follow:

### *Step 1:*

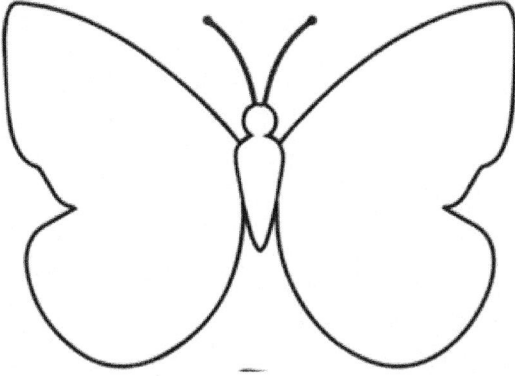

*Image 5.1: butterfly sketch*

First, draw the butterfly on either of the broadsides of the soapstone block. It doesn't have to be a perfect butterfly drawing, just a sketch to help you reduce the block into a basic butterfly shape as you start.

Make the sketch using a pencil until you achieve an illustration that can help you achieve a well-balanced butterfly carving like the one shown above (well-balanced means that the parts are proportional and wings are made equal on both sides).

### Step 2:

Once you have made the sketch, use the sculpting knife to re-draw the sketch's outer lines to give you a more permanent and visible mark. Remember, you can easily erase pencil marks with your hands by accident as you carve, hence losing track of the plan.

### Step 3:

*Image 5.2: basic shape of a soapstone butterfly*

After having the sketch, use the sculpting knife to shed off the outer part of the block following the sketch marks.

We are carving a small soapstone that doesn't require tools like a hammer and chisel. Since the block of soapstone is small, hold it in one hand as you chip away using the sculpting knife with the other hand.

Make single or two cuts, then turn to chip the other sides.

To make it a bit easier, chip away two opposite sides simultaneously, then move to the two other sides until you get a basic shape like the one shown above. As you can see, the soapstone is already reduced to a basic form of a butterfly.

**Note**: Do not worry about the antenna. We will use the thin wires later to represent them.

***Step 4:***

*Image 5.3: rasped basic shape of a soapstone butterfly*

At this point, we will use the rasps to:

• Smoothen the rough surface

• Make patterns on the butterfly where need be

- Reduce the basic shape into a more balanced one. As you saw in image 5:2 above, the wings are different in shape and size

- Work on the rough edges and corners

The rasps will reduce the basic shape into a more balanced form with patterns but still rough on the surface.

### Step 5:

From here, start refining the carving using sandpapers. Begin with the roughest sandpaper, and scrub the carving evenly, ensuring you do not overdo one side to maintain the shape.

As you sand the carving, occasionally feel the smoothness of the carving using your hand. This means that at some point, you will need to remove the glove, touch the surface of the carving, then continue.

Do the sanding as you change the sandpapers from the roughest to the finest before you move to wet sanding. At this stage, you can use three sandpapers with different roughness in each of the two rounds of sanding, making them a total of six sandpapers.

### Step 6:

After the two rounds of sanding, now move on to wet sanding. Since our butterfly carving is not large, do not fill your basin with water.

Immerse the butterfly in the water and give it time to absorb before sanding. Here, we shall use two different sandpapers, and you will not necessarily need to wear hand gloves.

Start sanding with the rougher sandpaper and sand the carving evenly. Once done, pick the smoother sandpaper and immerse it in the water to make it wet. Sand the carving as you observe it becoming marble-like smooth. Scrub the carving until you are happy with the result.

**Note:** As you carve, ensure that you optimize the use of your resources for economic purposes. Minimize waste as you maximize the utility of each material. For example, when making a small carving, pick small soapstone and not a huge one to the extent that what you will chip away is more than what will remain as the carving. Also, as in our case, filling your basin with water will be wasteful. Put just a little that is enough to cover your carving.

### Step 7:

Once you achieve your desired texture on the surface of the carving, rinse it to remove the gunk. Make two holes on the head (forehead) where you will put the thin wires as the antenna and allow the carving to dry.

### Step 8:

After it is dry, it is time to wax or oil it.

To do this:

Take some oil and rub it on the carving using your hand. Rub on the carving continuously as you add oil. Do not just apply the oil and leave it at that point. Continue rubbing since the carving needs the heat from the hand rubbing to absorb the oil.

Depending on the color of the stone you used, you will see a change in color as you continue applying the oil. In most cases, the color becomes denser or changes completely. Besides the color effect, the carving will give a mirror-like sparkle, making it more attractive.

## Step 9:

*Image 5.4: butterfly carving*

When you finish oiling, you can now put the antenna.

Cut two pieces out of the thin wire (3cm each). Put each in the two holes you made on the forehead of the butterfly and glue them. Then bend them towards the wings to make them look like the antenna.

After this, you can now start coloring your butterfly as you desire.

And guess what?

Congratulations!

You have successfully made your first soapstone carving. You found that very simple and probably didn't take much of your time, right?

Well, that's how simple it is to make a soapstone carving.

Moving on,

Let's try to curve something a little bigger!

# Chapter 7: How to Carve African Traditional Stool

An African-traditional stool is a beautiful chair that is a pure product of sculpting. Most common ones are carved from wood, but soapstone can also make a very nice one.

Even though these stools are made in unique designs with many modifications today, they were always made in three or four-legged forms.

And,

In our case, let's make a four-legged stool.

## Requirements:

✓ A block of chlorite soapstone (30cm by 30cm by 45cm),

✓ Chisel

✓ Hummers (a metallic head hammer and a wooden head hammer)

✓ Rasps

✓ Workbench

✓ Protective gear

- ✓ A sculpting knife

- ✓ Ruler or a meter rule

- ✓ Thin thread

- ✓ Two pieces of nails

- ✓ Pencil

- ✓ Basin

- ✓ Water

- ✓ Sandpapers

## Instructions

Unlike the butterfly we just made, which doesn't require much space, this stool will require a more expansive workspace with a workbench. This is because the carving we will make this time is enormous and cannot be carried while carving like the butterfly.

## Steps to Follow:

### *Step 1:*

Since you already have the block of soapstone, the next step is to prepare the workspace. First, choose the workspace and set your workbench in place. Assemble all your tools and put them in a strategic position, most preferably in a raised spot. If you use a room with raised fixtures and fittings, put your equipment in the fittings slightly above your workbench.

**NOTE**: In most cases, you will not find the soapstone in regular shapes, as we are assuming in our case here. So, if you have a soapstone with an irregular shape, you can either try to make it regular to ease your work when making the sketch or use it as it is.

### *Step 2:*

Place the soapstone block on the workbench and draw the sketch.

Our stool will have a round top with four legs. Using the meter rule and the pencil, draw the two diagonal lines on the top surface of the block. In our case, the top side should be one of the square sides. Where the diagonals intersect is the center of that surface.

Using the thread and the two nails, measure the optimal radius on the surface and draw the circle on the surface. The rope and the nail will give you a perfect ring.

Draw the circle repeatedly to ensure you have a more visible and hard-to-erase mark. Do the same with the bottom side.

### *Step 3:*

Put on the protective gears and start carving.

With the guidance of the top and bottom circular marks, reduce the cuboid soapstone into a cylindrical shape using the flatted chisel and the metallic head hammer. Chip away the corners and the other outer parts of the block until you get a cylindrical soapstone.

## *Step 4:*

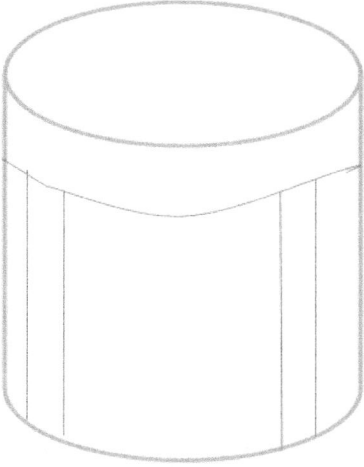

*Image 6.1: sketched cylindrical stone*

Using the pencil, sketch the stool's structure on the cylindrical soapstone, marking where the top part will meet the legs and positioning the four legs evenly around the cylinder.

As shown above, the sketch will guide you on continuing the chipping. But before chipping, space the four legs evenly around the cylinder for balance. Also, ensure that you allocate enough material for the top part of the stool. Then use the sculpting knife to affirm the sketch marks.

### Step 5:

Again, using the flatted chisel and the hammer, chip away the soapstone between the legs according to the sketch, not extending to the top part. Chip away all the sides simultaneously to ensure you don't eat into the legs on the sides of the stone.

### Step 6:

If you do this right, you will get a basic shape for the stool. Invert the chair with the top side on the bench to make it easy to shape the legs.

This time use the wooden hammer with the flatted chisel to shape the legs. This is because, at this stage, you will not need to chip away big piles of soapstone. Also, you must be more careful and gentle not to break the legs as you try to shape them.

### Step 7:

Once you get the basic shape of the legs, turn to the top part. Using the flat chisel and the wooden hammer still, chip away the inner part of the top to give you a shallow basin-like shape or a flat chapatti/roti pan shape.

Shape the stool's edges and corners using the diamond and corner chisels.

## Step 8:

After all this, your stool will have taken shape but with rough edges and surfaces. To reduce the roughness and make the chair look more in form, use the sculpting knife to slice thin pieces off the stool's surface. This will make the chair smoother and ready for rasps.

## Step 9:

As we did in the butterfly case, you start with the roughest rasp, moving to the smoother one until you get to the softest. But ensure that you rasp the whole stool evenly with every rasp texture to maintain the form.

## Step 10:

After the rasps, dust off the stool and start sanding. Again, start with the sandpaper with the roughest texture and rub the whole seat evenly. You can then now move to the smoother sandpaper up to the softest. Ensure you dust off the stool entirely before sanding it with the next smoother sandpaper.

***Step 11:***

Once you have sanded using all the different sandpapers, the next step is wet sanding.

Fill your basin with water, immerse the stool, and let it absorb moisture. Use wet sandpaper to sand the whole chair evenly.

A correctly done wet sanding will give you the smoothest surface, as soft as marble.

***Step 12:***

*Image 6.2: A traditional stool*

To this point, your soapstone-African stool will be ready for oiling, depending on where or how you will use it.

If the stool carving is for decoration and not for sitting on, then oiling is necessary to make it sparkle more. But if it is for sitting on, then oiling is not required.

**Note:**

✓ Chlorite soapstone is the most appropriate for the stool since it is expected to carry some weight. Talc soapstone will, therefore, not be applicable unless the stool carving is purely for decoration.

✓ Also, since the stool is likely to be moved from place to place more often, chlorite soapstone, the hardest soapstone, is the most appropriate.

✓ Ensure that your stool has fairly thick legs for longevity.

# Chapter 8: How to Create a Hawk Carving Using Electronic Tools

In the two exercises above, we have learned how to carve using hand tools. Now let's look at how to make a hawk carving using electronic instruments.

## Supplies:

- ✓ An irregularly shaped soapstone

- ✓ Variable speed angle grinder

- ✓ Variable speed die grinder

- ✓ Variable speed Dremel

- ✓ Diamond braised burrs (large sizes and small sizes for Dremel)

- ✓ Buffing wheels

- ✓ Boiled linseed oil

- ✓ Sintered cutter blades

- ✓ Braised diamond blades

- ✓ Sanding pads

# Instructions:

## *Step 1:*

Since we will be using irregularly shaped soapstone, the first step would be to inspect if the soapstone has any cracks.

To achieve this, you must eliminate the rough surface by sanding the whole soapstone to get a smooth surface that will let you see any crack easily. You do not want to carve with cracked soapstone, as that will eventually break and reduce the entire work to nothing.

So, to check for cracks:

Attach the sanding pad to the die grinder and set it to full speed. Give it time to reach full speed before you bring the rotating sanding pad into contact with the stone and start sanding it.

Do not press so hard on the soapstone.

Remove the parts if the stone has cracks to ensure you work on utterly intact soapstone.

### Step 2:

Once you have inspected the material and confirmed that it is fit for use, the next step is determining the positions of different carving parts.

Considering the shape of your soapstone, which side of the stone will be the head, the base, the top surface, and the tail?

This is the trickiest and most crucial part you should not overlook because if you don't do this right, you may have trouble shaping your bird.

### Step 3:

Following the typical shape of birds, you will want the narrow side of the stone to be the head and the wider side to make the tail. Then position the stone on the workbench with the side you want to be the top surface facing upwards.

I would advise starting with the head as you carve to get the basic shape.

So,

Using a pencil, mark the shape of the head on the material and start carving from there. How you position the head will determine how the rest of the body will be.

## Step 4:

At this stage, use the angle grinder with braised diamond blades.

Fix the braised diamond blade on the grinder, connect it to the power source, then switch it on. Since you are just starting the carving, it is advisable to use a lower speed to not over-cut the material.

Here, you are not making a perfect head yet but just shaping the material into a form that will give you an easier time positioning the rest of the body and shaping the head much more quickly. The product from this stage will therefore be more box-like.

## Step 5:

After the head, extending to the neck and the stomach towards the legs is easier. Sketch and chip away the soapstone to get the curve that runs from the head to the legs. Carefully do this as you relate to the remaining material on the upper part to accommodate the body.

Remember that your carving must be proportionate to represent the bird.

Also, ensure that you only extend the curve to the stomach to allow you to position the legs appropriately. If you stretch it further, you might go past where the legs should be, messing up the whole carving.

### Step 6:

After setting the lower curve, you can get to the top part.

Chip away the top part, making a curve that extends from the neck to the tail. At this stage, chip out thin slices of the soapstone on the top part and stop to check if the carving is in shape considering the lower curve.

Take your time to make the upper surface achieve a proportional figure.

### Step 7:

Once you have made the upper curve, shape the tail, extending it down towards the legs. Up to this point, you will remain with enough material to position the legs later.

It is advisable to return to shaping your carvings to look better before shaping their bases. And so, in this case, it would be best if you do not make the legs yet. Therefore, in the next step, start shaping the head and the rest of the body, then finish with the legs.

## *Step 8:*

From here, you must remove the diamond braised blade and attach the sintered cutter blade to do the shaping process. The advantage of this blade is that you cut and shape simultaneously. Using this blade, remove the sharp corners left by the former edge to make them curvy.

Also, use the variable speed die grinder at this stage.

On the head, you will use the variable speed die grinder more at this stage since the sintered blade has more friction that can easily break it. However, it is okay for the rest of the body.

Starting with the head, fix the diamond braised burr on the die grinder, connect it to the power source, and switch it on. Next, please set it to a medium speed and let it reach the whole set speed, then bring it into slight contact with the carving.

Move the grinder evenly to ensure a perfect, proportionate, well-positioned head.

When you are done with the head, extend to the lower curve, the upper part, and the rest of the body, then turn to shape the legs.

### Step 9:

To start making the legs, first, you must determine where to position them. You must carefully do this since the position of the legs will determine whether the hawk carving can attain balance and stand on its own.

Use the die grinder with burrs to make the basic leg shapes. This grinder is most appropriate since it can carve even to places where the angle grinder cannot reach.

As you make the legs, ensure that the front part joins with the back part of the hawk smoothly.

### Step 10:

Up to this point, you will have the complete shape of the hawk, but the surface is uniform and rough. Therefore, sanding becomes the next thing to do.

Remove the burr from the die grinder, fix sanding pads, and sand the whole carving to smooth the surface.

## Step 11:

Once you have made the whole surface smooth, it is time to make the finer details of the carving. This is the time when you will start using the Dremel.

To do this:

Fit a burr on the Dremel, switch it on, and start carving the finer parts of the hawk. Starting with the head, shape the beak, the eyes, and even the feathers if you wish to.

On the back, shape the wings and the feathers and extend to the tail. On the legs, you can make the scales; shape the foot and the claws.

## Step 12:

From here, the only remaining part is applying oil to the carving to make it sparkling and complete.

On the die grinder, replace the sanding pad with the buffing wheel. Get the carving ready for oiling by dusting it off. You can apply the oil by rubbing it on the carving with your hands or using a cloth to smear it. You will apply the oil to the die grinder with the buffing wheel.

So,

Switch on the die grinder and set it to a slow speed; pour a little oil on the carving and spread it throughout the carving using the rotating buffing wheel. Keep adding oil until the whole body is adequately covered.

### Step 13:

From there, you can decorate the carving by painting to distinguish several parts of the carving as you wish. And here you have a hawk carving.

The above projects are to help you get started with soapstone carving. After these successful projects, you probably are sure that soapstone carving is not intricate as you may have thought. With this motivation, pick an object of your choice and start carving.

Your first projects may not be as perfect as the ones that attracted you in the carving market, but with practice; you will get better until you can make the ideal carvings.

# Chapter 9: How to Carve a Soapstone Bear

## Supplies:

✓ Talc soapstone (30cm by 15cm by 15cm)

✓ Pencil

✓ A sculpting knife

✓ Chisels

✓ Wooden head hammer

✓ Rasps

✓ Sandpapers

✓ Variable speed Dremel

✓ Beeswax

✓ Water

✓ Basin

✓ Hand gloves

✓ Painting brush

# Instructions:

### *Step 1:*

Prepare your workspace by setting the workbench, placing the soapstone on it, and arranging your tools in a secure, easy-to-access area.

### *Step 2:*

*Image: 9.1: Sketch of a bear*

On one of the large sides of the soapstone (30cm by 15cm wide), sketch the bear's shape using a pencil. Using the sculpting knife, make the drawing more visible and permanent.

The sketch should be the outer lines of the bear's body and not a detailed drawing.

## Step 3:

Using the flat chisel and the hammer, chip away the material outside the sketch lines. You will get the bear's shape but with flat surfaces and sharp edges. Take the sculpting knife and start chipping away thin slices of the soapstone, beginning with the sharp edges until you get a basic round shape of the bear. It is at this stage that you shape the legs, the ears, and the head.

## Step 4:

After the sculpting knife, use the rasps to shape the parts more. Start with the roughest one, rasp the whole carving evenly, then move to a finer one and do the same to the finest rasp.

## Step 5:

When you finish rasping, dust off the carving and start sanding. Using the roughest sandpaper, sand the whole carving, move to finer sandpaper and sand the carving sequentially up to your finest sandpaper. By the time you finish the sandpapers, you will have removed the scratches left by the rasps.

**Step 6:**

Then, fill your basin with water and immerse the carving. Also, put the sandpaper(s) in the water to wet, ready for wet sanding. As we learned earlier, you can do this step using only one piece of sandpaper or, at most, two.

Wet sand the carving as you feel its surface with your hand. Sand it until its surface becomes as smooth as marble. Then let it dry.

**Step 7:**

Once the carving is dried, use the variable speed Dremel with burrs to make the finer details of the eyes, the nose, the fur on the body, and the feet.

**Step 8:**

*Image 9.2: Bear carving stages*

When you finish the finer details, put the carving in the oven and heat it to slightly above 100°C, say 120°C.

On the hot carving, put the beeswax and let the heat melt. Spread the wax on the body using the painting brush until the whole body is waxed. As you spread, ensure to distribute the polish on the carving evenly and that it is not waxed excessively.

Let the carving cool; the wax will make the carving sparkling and shiny.

And,

Just that simple, you will have made an attractive bear carving.

# Chapter 10: How to Make a Soapstone Cooking Pot

## Supplies:

- ✓ Chlorite soapstone (30cm by 30cm by 25cm)

- ✓ Variable speed die grinder

- ✓ Cutting blades

- ✓ A sculpting knife

- ✓ Meter rule

- ✓ Pencil

- ✓ Chisels

- ✓ Hammer

- ✓ Calipers

- ✓ Tung oil

- ✓ Geometric compass

- ✓ Sanding sponges (various roughnesses)

# Instructions:

## Step 1:

*Image 10.1:First circle on the surface of the soapstone block.*

Use the meter rule and the pencil to draw diagonals on the soapstone block's 30cm by 30cm two sides. Where the diagonals intersect is the center of the surface. Use the geometric compass to draw two circles on each side, 15cm and 13cm radii on both sides, using the intersection as the center.

The larger circle will make the outer side of the cooking pot, while the smaller one will be the inner side.

## Step 2:

Select two opposite corners of the soapstone and chip away the material using the die grinder with the cutting blades. This will leave you with a cylindrical block with two protruded sides. The two sides will help you create the handles.

### *Step 3:*

On the top side, shape the handles before you chip away the remaining part of the corners.

Using the chisels and the hammer, dig a hole inside the block, with the inner circle as the boundary line. Chip away the material in the cylindrical soapstone; be careful not to chip through to remove the bottom surface of the pot. You can leave a 2cm thickness for the bottom. Up to this point, you have the basic shape of the cooking pot.

### *Step 4:*

Once you have the basic shape, use the die grinder with the sanding sponges to sand the pot. Filing using the die grinder will be enough; wet sanding is unnecessary.

*Step 5:*

*Image 10.2: Soapstone cooking pot.*

After sanding, dust the pot off and use the Tung oil to polish the pot.

**Note:** It is not advisable to wax a cooking pot because wax melts when exposed to high temperatures.

# Chapter 11: Carving a Soapstone Tortoise

Soapstone tortoise carving makes a stunning decorative object. However, carving a tortoise might be tricky since you have to do it in three layers. It is one of the rare cases where you must start from the legs, contrary to what we learned earlier, but with the help of this book, you can create this masterpiece.

Let's have a look at what you need:

## Supplies:

✓ Talc soapstone (15cm by 12cm by 9cm)

✓ A sculpting knifes

✓ Rasps

✓ Sandpapers

✓ Boiled linseed oil

# Instructions:

## *Step 1:*

*Image 11.1: Outer sketch of a tortoise*

On one broadside of the soapstone, sketch the outline of the tortoise, as shown in the example above.

## *Step 2:*

After sketching, start by carving the legs. Ensure that the legs are on the edges of the soapstone. Once you have cut the four legs, outline the head positioning between the two front legs. Carve the head, ensuring that you position it slightly above the legs.

From there, outline the shell, which will be much easier since the head and the legs are already positioned. Carve and shape it properly; you now have a tortoise's basic shape.

### Step 3:

Using the sculpting knife and the rasps, add the details as you smoothen the edges.

### Step 4:

Dry sand and wet sand the tortoise until you get the surface smooth to your satisfaction.

### Step 5:

Let it dry, and apply the boiled linseed oil all over the carving using your hand, or you can use a piece of cloth to rub the oil on the carving.

## *Step 6:*

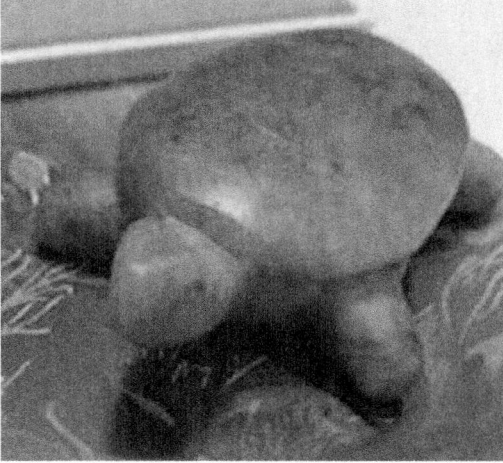

*Image 11.2: Tortoise soapstone carving*

Your tortoise carving is ready for further decoration if you wish to.

# Chapter 12: Carving a Soapstone Rabbit

## Supplies:

✓ Talc soapstone

✓ Pencil

✓ A sculpting knife

✓ Rasps

✓ Sandpapers

✓ Basin

✓ Water

✓ Linseed oil

# Instructions:

## Step 1:

*Image 12.1: Rabbit outline sketch*

First, sketch the rabbit's outline on the broad side of the soapstone using the pencil, then make them bold and permanent using the sculpting knife.

## *Step 2:*

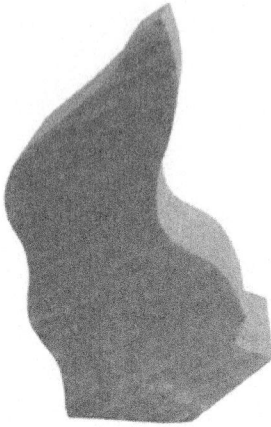

*Image 12.2: soapstone rabbit basic shape*

Using the sculpting knife, chip away the soapstone outside the sketch. Ensure that you do not chip into the line. Always leave a small allowance from the line for rasping and sanding. After chipping away the unwanted parts of the soapstone, you will remain with the basic shape shown above.

Shape the other parts, such as the ears and the legs, using the sculpting knife. Then, chip away thin slices off the sharp edges to give your rabbit a round shape.

### Step 3:

Once you have achieved a round shape, use the rasps to remove the rough surfaces and create fine details.

### Step 4:

Sand the carving until you do away with the scratches left by the rasps. Put the rabbit carving in the water basin, and immerse the sandpaper to make it wet. Sand the carving until you are happy with the product.

### Step 5:

Let it dry, and apply the linseed oil.

### Step 6:

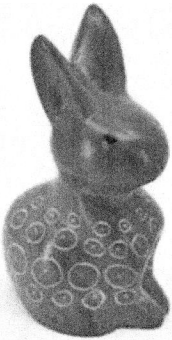

*Image 12.2: Decorated soapstone rabbit carving*

Decorate it as you wish.

# Chapter 13: Carving Soapstone Coasters

## Supplies:

- ✓ Variable speed angle grinder
- ✓ Variable speed die grinder
- ✓ Sanding pads
- ✓ A sculpting knife
- ✓ Cylindrical talc soapstone (small, say, a radius of 5cm)
- ✓ Bench vice
- ✓ Boiled linseed oil

## Instructions:

Carving soapstone coasters does not require much time. You can make several of them within no time.

### Step 1:

Using the variable speed angle grinder, cut the soapstone into pieces ( say slices of 1cm thickness) according to the marks you made on it. This will give you cylindrical portions of soapstone.

### Step 2:

Using the variable speed die grinder with sanding pads, sand both sides of the sliced pieces ensuring that you give them smooth edges.

### Step 3:

From this point, your coasters will be ready for oiling, or you can make decorative patterns on them if you wish to. If you make the patterns, you sand them again to smooth the surfaces.

### *Step 4:*

*Image 13.1: soapstone coasters*

After sanding, you apply the linseed oil to bring out the attractive color and make them sparkle.

And you are done; the coasters are ready!

# Chapter 14: Carving a Soapstone Egg

Soapstone eggs and spheres make perfect decorative objects.

Here is what you need and the steps to follow:

## Supplies:

✓ Cubic soapstone

✓ Flat chisel

✓ A sculpting knife

✓ Rasps

✓ Ruler

✓ Pencil

✓ Sandpapers

✓ Water in a basin

✓ Tung oil

# Instructions:

### Step 1:

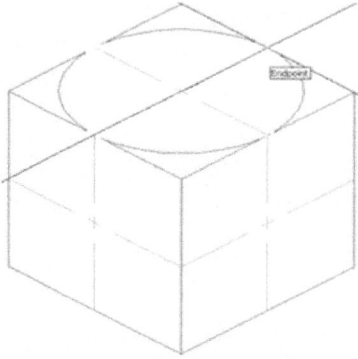

*Image 14.1: How to draw center lines on the soapstone cube*

On the cubic soapstone, draw the center lines and a circle on two opposite sides with a diameter equal to the cube's length.

### Step 2:

Chip away the corners, using the chisel, until you remain with cylindrical soapstone. Ensure that you do not erase the center lines at the top.

### Step 3:

Once you have the cylindrical shape, the next step is to shape the top and bottom parts of the cylinder from a circular shape to a curve shape. Up to this point, you will have oval-shaped soapstone.

Page | 110

### Step 4:

Using the sculpting knife, chip away thin slices of the soapstone evenly around the soapstone until you get the egg shape, which is an oval with one end smaller than the other.

### Step 5:

After getting this shape, use the rasps to make the egg more rounded.

### Step 6:

Then starting with the roughest sandpaper, sand the egg all around. Move to finer sandpaper and do the same until you get to the finest one. This first round of sanding will eliminate the roughness caused by the rasps.

### Step 7:

After the first sanding, you get to wet sanding. Put the soapstone egg into the water together with the sandpaper you want to use. Ensure that the sandpaper you use is either of equal fineness or finer than the last one you used in the dry sanding. Sand the egg as you feel with your hand until you are happy with how smooth the egg has become.

Let the carving dry.

## *Step 8:*

*Image 14.2: Soapstone egg*

When the carving is dry, apply the Tung oil.

Soapstone has beautiful veins that can serve as decoration. The Tung oil will make the veins more visible and sparkling, beautifying the soapstone egg without decorating it with paint.

# Chapter 15: Carving a Soapstone Candle Holder

You can make candle holders in various designs using soapstone. However, the distinction only comes on the stem, while the head and the base remain the same.

To make the handle:

## Supplies:

✓ Soapstone

✓ A sculpting knife

✓ Rasps

✓ Sandpaper

✓ Pencil

✓ Beeswax

# Instructions:

### *Step 1:*

On the soapstone, sketch the design of the candle stand you would like to make. Then, using the sculpting knife, carefully chip away the outer soapstone around the sketch. This will give you the basic shape of the holder you sketched.

### *Step 2:*

With the basic shape, continue chipping away the soapstone for a finer form. On the top side, dig a shallow hole that will hold the candle. Then use the rasp to shape it much better.

### *Step 3:*

After rasping, do two rounds of sanding.

## Step 4:

*Image 15.1: Soapstone candle holders*

After sanding, dry the carving up, put it in the oven, and heat it to 250 Degrees Celsius, then apply the beeswax.

Candle stands look better waxed than polished using oil.

# Conclusion

Acquiring soapstone carving skills is just as easy as you have learned. This book has reduced what you may have thought to be complicated into a few easy-to-follow steps in straightforward language. The whole idea is in carving and having the right tools for the job.

Being able to make attractive soapstone carvings is very fulfilling. But the knowledge alone is insufficient; you must keep practicing until you perfect it. And, with the growing market of sculpture products, this skill will save you money and might be the real deal earning you money.

Yes,

All you have to do now is to decide the next carving to make, assemble the tools and the materials, and get to work. But no matter the project you are working on, please ensure that you wear the proper safety gear, stay alert and follow the safety precautions.

All the best!

PS: I'd like your feedback. If you are happy with this book, please leave a review on Amazon.

Please leave a review for this book on Amazon by visiting the page below:

https://amzn.to/2VMR5qr

Printed in Great Britain
by Amazon